Folk Art
on
Terracotta
Eva Tummel

Kangaroo Press

I dedicate this book to my fellow artist and folk art teacher—but most of all my best friend—my daughter Nicole!

—Love, Mum

Introduction

Bauernmalerei or 'farmers' painting' is a traditional European art, dating back to the seventeenth or eighteenth century. We refer to it today in general terms as folk art.

In Germany we find *Bauernmalerei*, in France *Tole* painting, in Holland *Hindeloopen*, in Norway *Rosemaling*. There are also the beautiful traditions of Hungary, Austria and Bavaria, and of Russian folk art.

There are large variations in designs, styles and colour combinations from country to country, and between different districts and villages. In most parts of Europe designs and techniques have been handed down from generation to generation, thus developing unique regional styles.

I spent most of my childhood in Europe, so my love for folk art goes back a long way. As a teenager I studied commercial and advertising art in Australia, and worked for twenty-five years designing greeting cards for a number of publishers.

Folk art has always been my favourite pastime. I introduced it to my friends and students in the early 1960s, painting small gifts for my friends and family, children's furniture, wooden articles large and small. This beautiful unpretentious art can transform and add beauty to any home. It works on wood, tin, terracotta, glass—even on fabric.

I have been teaching folk art, the traditional *Bauernmalerei*, for many years in Victoria and South Australia, and for the past seven years in Queensland. The last few years I have also started to teach folk art with Australian flowers.

Bauernmalerei is mostly applied to wood or tin, but it looks great on terracotta! My students' favourite lessons are on terracotta pots and plates. In this book I would like to pass on to you my ideas, patterns and colour combinations to make the most of your terracotta items. It was my personal choice to base-coat most of the terracotta items, but all the projects and patterns look very good on plain terracotta as well! Do experiment with other base-coat colours.

To paint on terracotta is fun and economical. The items are useful and very decorative. I have included on some projects my rose design, and the forget-me-not, my favourite little flower which has been my trademark for many years. I do hope you will get a lot of pleasure from the projects in this book.

Happy painting!

Front cover: Terracotta basket, soap dish, potpourri dish, picture and frame offer a variety of possibilities for gift giving

Back cover: A detailed traditional urn of flowers enlivens the simple shape of the lamp base (page 8). Elements of the large design appear on the pretty scalloped pot (page 10)

© Eva Tummel 1993

Reprinted in 1994 and 1996
First published in 1993 by Kangaroo Press Pty Ltd
3 Whitehall Road Kenthurst NSW 2156 Australia
P.O. Box 6125 Dural Delivery Centre NSW 2158
Printed in Hong Kong through Colorcraft Ltd

ISBN 0 86417 520 5

Project Preparation

Preparation before painting your projects is very important in achieving a well finished product. Use these techniques for preparing and base-coating terracotta:

Terracotta (natural):
1. Clean terracotta article thoroughly. If you use a damp cloth to remove dust and dirt, make sure you dry the article well before proceeding with painting.
2. Sand lightly with wet-and-dry sandpaper, wipe off any dust with lint-free cloth.
3. Trace design from book onto tracing paper with 2B pencil.
4. Position design on terracotta item, placing white or black transfer paper between tracing paper and project.
5. Retrace design with 5H pencil. You might have to cut the pattern in half and trace one half first, then the other, as most items are rounded, making it harder to transfer designs. Try to freehand some of the designs.
6. Project is now ready to paint. Follow painting guide for each project.

Note:
1. You can paint straight onto terracotta.
2. You can paint terracotta with one coat of all-purpose sealer before painting.
3. You can add a few drops of sealer to each colour.

Terracotta (coloured background):
Base coat
First coat: 1 part paint + 1 part all-purpose sealer.
Second coat: Paint only!
1. Clean terracotta article thoroughly. If you use a damp cloth to remove dust and dirt, make sure you dry the article well before proceeding with base-coat colour.
2. Sand lightly with wet-and-dry sandpaper, wipe off any dust with lint-free cloth.
3. Apply first coat of base-coat colour mixed with all-purpose sealer using ½" flat brush or #12 round brush. Let dry well before applying second coat of colour.
4. Paint second coat of base-coat colour, this time paint only! (If third coat is necessary for better coverage apply paint only.)

5. Trace design from book onto tracing paper with 2B pencil.
6. Position design on terracotta item, placing white or black transfer paper between tracing paper and project.
7. Retrace design with 5H pencil. Try to freehand some of the designs.
8. Project is now ready to paint. Follow painting guide for each project.

Crackling: When using crackle medium you must work fast, as crackle medium won't work after 24 hours. This means you must finish the project in one day.
1. After cleaning terracotta article, paint with one coat of base-coat colour mixed with sealer, let dry. Next, apply in rapid succession four coats of base-coat colour, this time paint only! Let dry between coats.
2. Trace design onto article and paint. Designs for these articles should be simple so you can paint them on in a short time.
3. As soon as design is dry, apply thick coat of crackle medium all over article.
4. Place in a warm area (under a desk light is ideal). Within 20 minutes small cracks will appear. Do not use hairdryer!

Stain: After crackling your article apply stain.
To mix stain: 1 part paint (Brown or Burgundy)
              1 part retarder and some water
              1 part sealer
Mix together—don't make stain too dark.
1. Apply stain all over project with ½" flat brush.
2. Wipe off excess stain with a soft lint-free cloth. If stain dries too fast dampen the cloth and wipe over again, leaving stain only in cracks and just a touch over the rest of the project to give it an antique look.
3. After stain is dry, apply 2 coats of varnish, following instructions for varnishing.

N.B. No responsibility is taken by the artist or the publishers of this book for any articles spoiled due to using inferior materials or not taking proper care.

Materials

Paints: Waterbased acrylic paints (artists' colours). As there are at least 5 different brands of paints presently on the market, I leave the choice to you. To match colours, ask for a colour chart. There are 50 to 120 different colours available in most brands; from those you can mix at least another 50 shades. Decorative colours come in 50 ml bottles or 75 ml tubes.
Base-coat colours come in 250 ml bottles or jars.

Varnishes: Waterbased polyurethane varnish (non-yellowing), available in satin or gloss finish in 250 ml bottles.
Use soft fibre flat brush ½'' or 1'' wide. Apply varnish with even strokes in one direction only! Try not to go over the same strokes again. On most articles two coats of varnish are sufficient. You may apply three or four coats of varnish for extra gloss and durability. Avoid varnishing in a draught or in front of a fan.

All-purpose sealer: A very important medium which should be used in all base-coat colours. If you prefer to leave the terracotta a natural colour you must first seal it with all-purpose sealer, let it dry, then sand lightly and proceed with painting.

With any brand of paint, varnish or sealer follow manufacturer's instructions on drying period and make sure the materials you use are non toxic!

Brushes: Good quality synthetic fibre or synthetic sable. (Acrylic paints will ruin pure sable brushes very quickly.) Brushes used for projects in this book: #00, #1, #2, #4, #6 round brushes. Flat brush ½'' wide for base-coating, flat brush 1'' for varnishing.

Brush care: Rinse your brushes frequently in cold water during painting. After finishing a project, rinse your brush in soapy water—this will prevent paint building up in the ferrule (near metal part of brush). To maintain good points on brushes, roll them in ordinary toilet soap, shape into a fine point and stand upright in a jar or brush holder. Before use rinse soap out in cold water.

Terracotta articles: Ducks, geese, plates, etc. For information on supply of terracotta articles and Country Folk Art Club Membership write to: Mrs Eva Tummel, 'Folklore House', PO Box 646, Nambour 4560 Qld. Australia.

Palette: Round palette (ten small dishes and one large in centre).

Pencils: 2B for drawing and tracing patterns.
5H for transferring design onto project
White, black or peach coloured carbon pencil for freehand drawing.

Tracing paper, rubber and transfer paper: Black, white or yellow.

Sketch pad: Practice your strokes and colour combinations.

Sandpaper: Wet-and-dry sandpaper #400 or #600.

And: Water jar to rinse your brushes in. Spray mist bottle to moisten the paint occasionally, preventing it from drying up. Freezer bag to cover your palette, preserving paint in between use. Paints in palettes will last for weeks if you look after them!

Finishes: Every project completed must have a good finish—without that your work is incomplete. Paint front, back, sides and insides of projects! Varnish all your projects—it will protect them from dust and dirt, and also highlight the colours used for painting.

To store leftover or excess paint, use small airtight jars or plastic film canisters. Leftover paint also can be used for base-coating smaller articles, small pots, base-coating small ducks, painting insides of terracotta pots.

Wine cooler set (pages 11–13) decorated with apples, pears, grapes and strawberries

A delightful family of terracotta pigs bright with flowers (opposite)

Terracotta Pigs

(illustrated opposite)

Materials

Terracotta pigs.

Paints: Waterbased acrylics
Brushes: #6, #4, #2, #00 round brushes
   ½'' or 1'' flat brush
Tracing paper, black transfer paper
Varnish: Polyurethane gloss finish
Pencils: 2B and 5H
Sandpaper: Wet-and-dry #400 or #600

Palette

Base coat: Mushroom pink
Leaves: Dark green + white
Tulips: Medium yellow + white
Daisies: Medium yellow + white
Large flowers: Antique blue + white
Flower centres: Yellow + white + brown
Small flowers, dots: White
Hearts: Dark pink
Cheeks, nose: Soft pink
Eyes: Black

Preparation

Refer to page 3.

Painting guide

1. *Leaves:* Double load #4 brush with dark green and white, paint all leaves and comma strokes.
2. *Flowers:* For tulips and daisies use #6 brush, double load yellow and white.
3. *Blue flowers:* Use #6 or #4 brush, double load with blue and white.
4. *Flower centres:* With #2 brush paint centres yellow and white, add small brown dots with #00 brush to highlight centre.
5. *Hearts:* Paint with #4 brush, straight colour.
6. *Dots:* Paint white with #2 brush.
7. *Cheeks and nose:* Paint with #4 brush, soft pink.
8. *Eyes:* Eyes are usually already painted on terracotta items; if not, paint eyes black.
9. *Small pigs:* For painting designs use #2 and #00 brushes.
10. *Crackling:* Apply crackle medium all over pigs.
11. *Stain:* Apply stain, wipe off excess stain.

For crackling and staining techniques refer to page 3.

Finish

Apply 1 coat of gloss finish polyurethane varnish with 1'' flat brush. Let dry, preferably overnight. Apply second coat of varnish. Sand gently between coats.

Lamp Base

(illustrated on back cover)

Materials

Terracotta lamp base.

Paints: Waterbased acrylics

Brushes: #6, #4, #2, #00 round brushes
½'' and 1'' flat brushes

Tracing paper, white transfer paper

Varnish: Polyurethane satin finish

Pencils: 2B and 5H

Sandpaper: Wet-and-dry #400 or #600

Palette

Base coat: Turquoise

Leaves: Dark green—solid green
Light green + white

Large flowers: Dark pink, light pink + white

Small flowers: White, centres dark pink

Comma strokes: White—some dark green

Urn: Brown + white
Dots: White
Commas: Dark green

Preparation

Refer to page 3.

Painting guide

1. *Leaves:* Paint all dark green leaves in straight colour with #4 and #2 brushes. Light green leaves: double load #4 and #2 brushes with light green and white. Paint all light green leaves and comma strokes.
2. *Large flowers:* Paint soft pink flowers first with #4 and #2 brush. Paint medium pink flowers with #6 or #4 brush, double load with medium pink and white. Dark pink on flowers (straight pink) use #4 and #2 brush; for dots #00 brush.
3. *White flowers:* With #2 brush paint all flowers and comma strokes.
4. *White flower centres:* Dark pink, use #2 brush.
5. *Dots:* Large dots, small dots, paint white with #00 brush.
6. *Urn:* Double load #4 brush with brown and white, paint urn.
   Paint small lines with #00 brush.
   Paint all dots white with #00 brush.
   Outline urn with dark green, using #00 brush.
   Comma strokes, paint dark green with #00 brush.

Finish

Apply 1 coat of satin finish polyurethane varnish with 1'' flat brush. Let dry, preferably overnight. Apply second coat of varnish.

Scalloped Pot

(illustrated on front cover)

Materials

Terracotta scalloped pot.

Paints: Waterbased acrylics
Brushes: #2, #1, #00 round brushes
   ½'' and 1'' flat brushes
Tracing paper, white transfer paper
Varnish: Polyurethane satin finish
Pencils: 2B and 5H
Sandpaper: Wet-and-dry #400 or #600

Palette

Base coat: Turquoise
Leaves: Dark green—solid green
   Light green + white
Large flowers: Dark pink, light pink + white
Small flowers: White, centres dark pink
Comma strokes: White—some dark green
Dots: White—some pink

Preparation

Refer to page 3.

Painting guide

1. *Leaves:* Paint all dark green leaves in straight colour with #1 brush.
   Light green leaves: use #2 brush, double load with light green and white.
2. *Large flowers:* Paint soft pink flowers first with #2 brush, then double load with pink and white. Paint medium pink with #2 brush, double load with white. Dark pink—some solid pink, others double load with white.
3. *Small flowers:* White, dark pink centres, use #1 brush.
4. *Dots:* White—some pink—paint with #00 brush.

Finish

Apply 1 coat of satin finish polyurethane varnish with 1'' flat brush. Let dry, preferably overnight. Apply second coat of varnish.

Wine Cooler Set

(illustrated on page 5)

These designs appear on pages 12 and 13.

Materials
Terracotta wine cooler, plate and bowl.

Paints: Waterbased acrylics
Brushes: #6, #4, #2, #00 round brushes
    ½'' and 1'' flat brushes
Tracing paper, white transfer paper
Varnish: Polyurethane gloss finish
Pencils: 2B and 5H
Sandpaper: Wet-and-dry #400 or #600

Palette
Base coat: Black
Leaves: Dark green, yellow, white, brown
Apples: Dark red, light red, yellow, white
Pears: Yellow, white, green and orange
Grapes: Dark blue, purple and white
Strawberries: Dark red, medium red, white, yellow and
    brown
Curlicues: Rich gold

Preparation
Refer to page 3.

Painting guide
1. *Leaves:* Paint all leaves with dark green, a touch of yellow and a touch of brown. Triple load the three colours, using #6 round brush.
2. *Apples:* With #6 brush paint apples with brush double loaded with dark red and light red. Then add touches of yellow and white to highlight apples. Add a touch of brown near stem.
3. *Pears:* Double load #6 brush with yellow and white, paint pears. Add touches of green and orange, then highlight with white. Add a touch of brown near stem.
4. *Grapes:* With #4 brush paint grapes, first with dark blue and a touch of white. Add purple and finally white to highlight grapes. Diox purple gives the best results.
5. *Strawberries:* Double load #4 brush with dark red and light red, paint strawberries. Add white on outer edges, then yellow to highlight berries.
6. *Seeds:* Paint white and yellow teardrops, adding a touch of brown on one side of teardrops only—use #00 brush.
7. *Curlicues:* Paint curlicues gold, using #00 brush.

Finish
Apply 1 coat of gloss finish polyurethane varnish with 1'' flat brush. Let dry, preferably overnight. Apply second coat of varnish.

Handy hints
When painting on dark backgrounds—black, green, dark blue and burgundy—I advise you to base-coat all your leaves, fruits, and flowers (for example, leaves dark green, pears yellow, apples dark red) otherwise your designs will be transparent. Let dry, then proceed with painting instruction.

Always paint all the leaves first on the three articles, then all the apples, all the pears, etc.—you will get much better results.

Paint the wine cooler and bowl inside as well and varnish them the same way as the outside. Make sure the varnish you use is safe to serve food products on.

Please note: These articles are not dishwasher proof—hand wash only, or wipe off any marks with a damp cloth and dry.

Wine Cooler Set

Painting instructions on page 11.

Wine Cooler Set

Painting instructions on page 11.

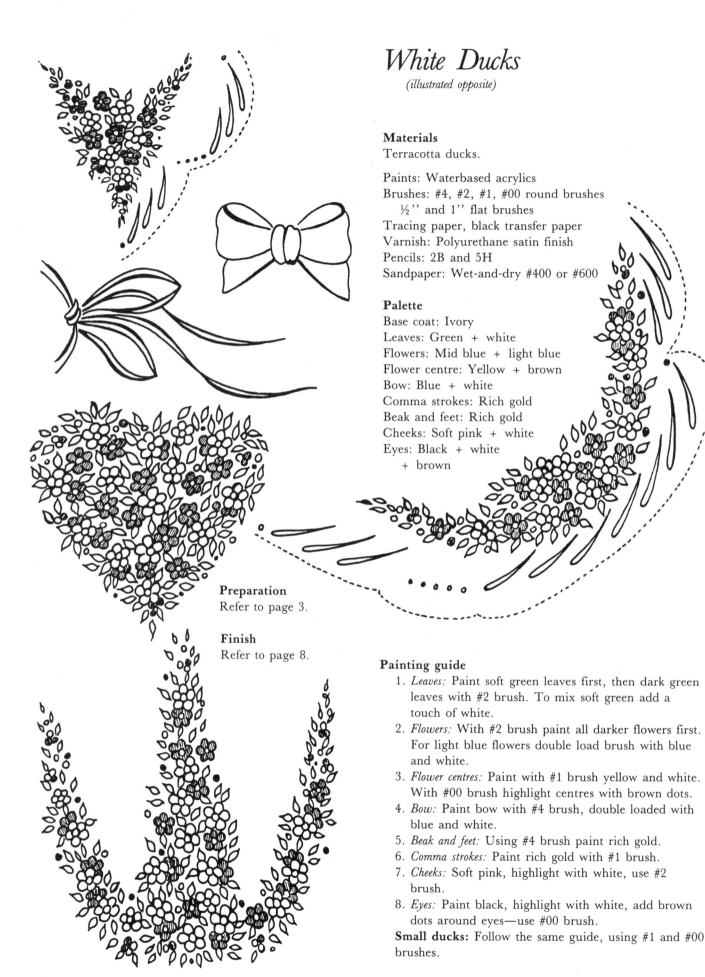

White Ducks
(illustrated opposite)

Materials
Terracotta ducks.

Paints: Waterbased acrylics
Brushes: #4, #2, #1, #00 round brushes
   ½'' and 1'' flat brushes
Tracing paper, black transfer paper
Varnish: Polyurethane satin finish
Pencils: 2B and 5H
Sandpaper: Wet-and-dry #400 or #600

Palette
Base coat: Ivory
Leaves: Green + white
Flowers: Mid blue + light blue
Flower centre: Yellow + brown
Bow: Blue + white
Comma strokes: Rich gold
Beak and feet: Rich gold
Cheeks: Soft pink + white
Eyes: Black + white
   + brown

Preparation
Refer to page 3.

Finish
Refer to page 8.

Painting guide

1. *Leaves:* Paint soft green leaves first, then dark green leaves with #2 brush. To mix soft green add a touch of white.
2. *Flowers:* With #2 brush paint all darker flowers first. For light blue flowers double load brush with blue and white.
3. *Flower centres:* Paint with #1 brush yellow and white. With #00 brush highlight centres with brown dots.
4. *Bow:* Paint bow with #4 brush, double loaded with blue and white.
5. *Beak and feet:* Using #4 brush paint rich gold.
6. *Comma strokes:* Paint rich gold with #1 brush.
7. *Cheeks:* Soft pink, highlight with white, use #2 brush.
8. *Eyes:* Paint black, highlight with white, add brown dots around eyes—use #00 brush.

Small ducks: Follow the same guide, using #1 and #00 brushes.

White ducks and ducklings richly decorated with tiny flowers
(opposite)

Brush Strokes - Leaves
Double Loading Technique

Rose Bud Leaves

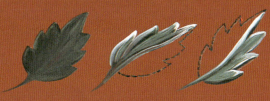

Strawberry

Violet Leaves

Roses

Trees

Cottage

Strawberry

Strawberry Flower

Tulip

Tulip leaves

Brush Strokes–Flowers
Double Loading Technique

Rose Buds

"Eva's Rose"

Violets

Forget-me-not

Traditional Rose

Daisies

Double Bow

Grapes

Pears

Apples

A feast of gold—a golden duck and a golden goose (pages 20–21) and a golden egg (opposite)

The Golden Egg

(illustrated opposite)

Materials
Terracotta egg.

Paints: Waterbased acrylics
Brushes: #4, #2, #1, #00 round brushes
  ½'' and 1'' flat brushes
Tracing paper, black transfer paper
Varnish: Polyurethane satin finish
Pencils: 2B and 5H
Sandpaper: Wet-and-dry #400 or #600

Palette
Base coat: Rich gold
Leaves: Dark green + gold
Roses: Dark pink + white
Scenery: Sky—blue + grey + white
  Mountains, grass—Dark green + light green
  River—Blue + white
Path: Brown
Flowers: Yellow + pink + white
Cottage: White + grey + dark pink + brown
Trees: Dark green + grey + white

Preparation
Refer to page 3.

Painting guide
Divide egg into 4 sections. Paint rose design first and large rose on top of egg, using #2 brush. Painting guide for roses is on page 20.

Paint ovals for the four seasons first, in grey, then follow instructions for each season. For scenery use #1 and #00 round brushes.

Summer
Sky: Blue + white
Mountains: Dark green + light green
Grass, Trees: Dark green + light green
River: Blue + white
Path: Brown
Flowers: Yellow + pink + white
Cottage: White + grey + orange + brown

Autumn
Sky: Blue + white
Mountains: Green + yellow
Grass, Trees: Green + yellow
River: Blue + white
Path: Brown
Cottage: White + grey + brown

Winter
Sky: Blue + grey + white
Mountains: Grey + white
Trees: Green + white
Ground: Grey + white
River: Blue + white + grey
Path: Brown
Cottage: White + brown
White spots for snowflakes

Spring
Sky: Blue + grey
Mountains: Blue + grey + white on top
Grass: Green.
Trees: Green + dark green
River: Blue + white
Path: Brown
Cottage: Grey + white + dark pink
  + brown

Golden Duck and Golden Goose

(illustrated on page 18)

Materials

Terracotta duck, goose and egg.

Paints: Waterbased acrylics
Brushes: #4, #2, #1, #00 round brushes
    ½'' and 1'' flat brush
Tracing paper, transfer paper
Varnish: Polyurethane satin finish
Pencils: 2B and 2H
Sandpaper: Wet-and-dry #400 or #600

Palette

Base coat: Rich gold
Leaves: Green + gold
Roses: Antique pink + white
Eyes: Black

Preparation

Refer to page 3.

Painting guide

1. *Leaves:* Paint all leaves with #2 brush, double loaded with green and rich gold.
2. *Stems and comma strokes:* Use #00 brush for small leaves and stems, also for comma strokes. Paint with straight green colour.
3. *Scallops:* Paint dark green with #4 brush.
4. *Roses:* With #4 brush first paint roses in solid colour (dark pink) and let dry. Then double load brush with pink and white, paint strokes over dark pink base coat as illustrated on centre page. Make sure they don't touch, and show a bit of the dark pink between each brush stroke.
5. *Smaller roses:* Paint centre design with #2 or #1 brush.
6. *Eyes:* Paint black with #1 brush. Most terracotta ducks have their eyes already painted.

Note

Materials, Palette, Preparation, Painting Guide and Finish are the same for both the Golden Duck and Golden Goose. Pattern on page 21 fits both articles.

Finish

Apply 1 coat of satin finish polyurethane varnish with 1'' flat brush. Let dry, preferably overnight. Apply second coat of varnish.

Golden Duck and Golden Goose

(illustrated on page 18)

Pattern for Golden Duck and Golden Goose

Large Terracotta Plate

(illustrated inside front cover)

Materials

Large terracotta plate.

Paints: Waterbased acrylics
Brushes: #6, #4, #2, #1, #00 round brushes
    ½'' and 1'' flat brushes
Tracing paper, transfer paper
Varnish: Polyurethane satin finish
Pencils: 2B and 5H
Sandpaper: Wet-and-dry #400 or #600

Palette

Leave plate natural colour.
Leaves: Dark Green + yellow + brown
Tulips: Golden brown + ivory
Roses: Deep orange + brown + ivory
Carnation: Deep orange + ivory
Daisies: Blue + ivory + yellow + brown

Preparation

Refer to page 3.

Painting guide

On page 23.

Small Terracotta Plate

(illustrated inside front cover)

Painting guide
FOR LARGE TERRACOTTA PLATE ON PAGE 22

1. *Leaves:* Paint all leaves with #6 brush, triple loaded in green, yellow and brown.
2. *Tulips:* Double load #6 brush with golden brown and ivory, paint all tulips.
3. *Roses:* With #4 brush paint dark brown centres and all four petals on each rose. Then double load #6 brush with dark orange and ivory, paint bowl part of roses. Lastly paint comma strokes on petals—double load with same colours, adding a touch more ivory this time. Paint the two centre strokes the same. Dots in ivory, using #2 brush.
4. *Carnations:* Double load #2 brush with dark orange and ivory, paint outer petals first.
5. *Daisies:* Using #4 brush for petals, double load blue and ivory, paint all daisies.
6. *Daisy centres:* With #1 brush paint them yellow and ivory; add fine brown dots with #00 brush.
7. *Commas and scrolls:* Double load dark green and yellow, paint with #2 and #1 brush.

Finish
Apply 1 coat of satin finish polyurethane varnish with 1'' flat brush. Let dry, preferably overnight. Apply second coat of varnish.

Painting guide
FOR SMALL TERRACOTTA PLATE
Materials
Same as large plate.
Brushes: #2, #1, #00 round brushes

Preparation
Refer to page 3.

Palette
Leave plate natural colour.
Faces: Flesh colour
Hair: Yellow
Skirt and pants: Yellow
Apron top and vest: Bright red
Blouse, socks, collar: White
Apron, coat, hats: Dark green + black
Shoes: Brown or black
Hearts: Bright red
Flowers: Dark blue + yellow
Leaves, commas: Dark green
Dots: White + rich gold

Painting guide
1. *Faces:* Paint flesh colour with #2 brush.
2. *Hair, skirt, pants, flowers:* Yellow with #2 brush. You might need two coats.
3. *Blouse, socks, collars and dots:* Paint white with #2 and #1 brush.
4. *Hats, apron, jacket, leaves:* Dark green, paint with #2, #1 and #00 brushes.
5. *Vest, front of apron:* Bright red, #2 brush.
6. *Heart, mouth:* Bright red, #2 and #00 brushes.
7. *Cheeks:* Soft red, fine dots—use #00 brush.
8. *Eyes and shoes:* Brown, use #1 and #00 brushes.
9. *Lines and dots:* Paint black with #00 brush.
10. Highlight design with rich gold.

Finish
Same as large terracotta plate.

Cream Cans

Cream Cans

(illustrated on page 27)

Materials
Terracotta cream cans with lids.

Paints: Waterbased acrylics
Brushes: #6, #4, #2, #1, #00 round brushes
    ½'' and 1'' flat brushes
Tracing paper, transfer paper
Varnish: Polyurethane gloss finish
Pencils: 2B and 5H
Sandpaper: Wet-and-dry #400 or #600

Palette
For all three cans and lids.
Base coat: Burgundy + brown + rich gold
Rose leaves: Dark green + cream
Roses, rosebuds: Burgundy + brown + cream
Scenery: Sky—Blue + grey + white
    Mountains, Grass—Dark green + light green +
      brown
    Trees—Dark green + brown + black
    Houses—Burgundy + brown + cream
    Sheep—White + black
Scrolls, handles: Rich gold

Preparation
Refer to page 3.

Painting guide
ROSES

1. *Leaves:* Paint all leaves with dark green, then double load with green and cream using #2 and #00 brushes. Some leaves are green only.
2. *Roses:* Paint dark centres and outer petals first with burgundy and touch of brown; use #2 brush for larger roses, for buds #1 or #00 brushes. Double load with burgundy and cream, paint centre part of rose first, then outer petals.
3. *Scrolls:* Paint with #00 brush in rich gold.

Painting guide
SCENERY

1. *Sky:* Double load #6 brush with blue and grey, paint sky, highlight with white. Use slight dry-brush effect near edges to let background colour come through.
2. *Mountains and grass:* Using #6 brush, double load with dark green and light green. Paint the whole area first, then add a touch of brown on some parts and touches of cream or grey to highlight mountains and grass.
3. *Trees:* Double load #4 or #2 brush with dark green and light green. Paint foliage with stippled effect, adding a touch of brown as well. Tree trunks are in brown and black—use #1 brush.
4. *Houses:* No. 1—Paint walls first with #2 brush in burgundy and brown, then paint roof brown, adding a touch of black as well. Windows, doors, cream with a touch of brown.
   No. 2—Walls are grey and white—double load #2 or #1 brush. Roof is burgundy and brown. Paint windows and doors with burgundy and brown, using #00 brush.
5. *Sheep:* Paint white with #00 brush; ears, legs, nose with black.
6. *Handles:* On cans and lids, paint with #4 brush in rich gold—use dry brush effect to let the burgundy colour come through slightly. It will give an old effect.

Finish
Apply 1 coat of gloss finish polyurethane varnish with 1'' flat brush. Let dry, preferably overnight. Apply second coat of varnish.

Cream can patterns See page 24. Use same pattern for medium and large cans, enlarging sky and grass areas.

Most terracotta jars and cans are glazed inside. If yours are not, paint the insides with colour and varnish the same as the outside. If you intend using jars or cans for food products, do make sure the paints and varnish you use are safe for storing food products.

Utensil Holder
(illustrated opposite)

Materials
Terracotta can without lid.

Paints: Waterbased acrylics
Brushes: #6, #4, #2, #1, #00 round brushes
½'' and 1'' flat brushes
Tracing paper, transfer paper
Varnish: Polyurethane gloss finish
Pencils: 2B and 5H
Sandpaper: Wet-and-dry #400 or #600

Preparation
Refer to page 3.

Painting guide for roses is the same as on cream cans (refer to page 25).

Palette

FIGURES	SCENERY
Faces: Flesh colour	Base coat: Burgundy
Hair: Yellow + brown	+ cream
Eyes: Blue.	Scenery: Sky—Blue
Mouth: Red.	+ grey + white
Tiara: Burgundy + green	Meadow & Hills—Dark
Blouse, apron, socks,	green + light green
collar: White	+ brown
Skirt, pants, shoes, hat:	Trees (comma strokes):
Black	Dark green + gold
Shirt: Blue + grey	Comma strokes: Rich
Vest, braces: Burgundy	gold
Buttons: Rich gold	Stick rose: Burgundy
	+ cream

Finish
Refer to page 25.

Painting guide
SCENERY
1. *Sky:* Double load #6 brush with blue and grey, paint sky, highlight with white.
2. *Meadow and hills:* With #6 brush paint dark green and light green—double load—then add a touch of brown and highlight with grey.
3. *Trees:* With #1 and #00 brush paint all comma strokes dark green—straight colour. Comma strokes near couple's feet are dark green double loaded with gold—use #1 brush.
4. *Stick roses:* Paint half of circle with burgundy, the other half with cream. Take a pencil and twirl the two colours together. Don't press too hard, or pencil marks will show.
5. *Commas on tree:* Rich gold; paint with #1 brush.

Painting guide
COUPLE
1. *Faces:* Paint faces, arms, hands with flesh colour, use #1 brush.
2. *Hair:* Double load yellow with brown, paint with #1 brush.
3. *Eyes and mouth:* Paint eyes blue, mouth red with #00 brush; pink cheeks.
4. *Paint all white areas* first with #2 and #1 brushes; you might need two coats of white to get good coverage.
5. *Black:* Paint all black areas next—skirt, pants, shoes, etc.—use #2 brush.
6. *Shirt:* Paint blue first, then add fine grey stripes with #00 brush.
7. *Vest, braces, flowers on girl's tiara:* Paint burgundy with #1 and #00 brushes. For the small leaves in green, use #00 brush.
8. *Details in apron and socks:* Light blue with #00 brush.
9. *Roses in skirt:* Pink and green, paint with #00 brush.
Handles: Rich gold, same as on cream cans.

26

Cream cans (page 25) and utensil holder (opposite) make a harmonious grouping

Cheerful teddy bear cookie jars (opposite) could find many alternative lives around the home

Teddy Bear Cookie Jars

(illustrated opposite)

Materials

Terracotta teddy bear cookie jars.

Paints: Waterbased acrylics
Brushes: #4, #2, #1, #00 round brushes
  ½'' and 1'' flat brushes
Tracing paper, transfer paper
Varnish: Polyurethane gloss finish
Pencils: 2B and 5H
Sandpaper: Wet-and-dry #400 or #600

Palette

Base coat: 1 bear pastel pink
  1 bear pastel blue
Bow and pads: Cream, also around eyes
Rosebuds: Pastel pink + cream
Hearts: Pastel pink
Leaves: Pale green + cream
Eyes: Brown + black + white
Nose: Brown + white

Preparation

Refer to page 3.

Painting guide

1. *Bears:* Paint one bear pink and the other bear blue with ½'' flat brush.

Finish

Apply 1 coat of gloss finish polyurethane varnish with 1'' flat brush. Let dry, preferably overnight. Apply second coat of varnish.

Note

Please make sure that terracotta bear cookie jars are glazed inside when you purchase them, especially if they will be used for food products. The jars can also be used as money boxes, or for cotton balls in bathrooms or children's rooms.

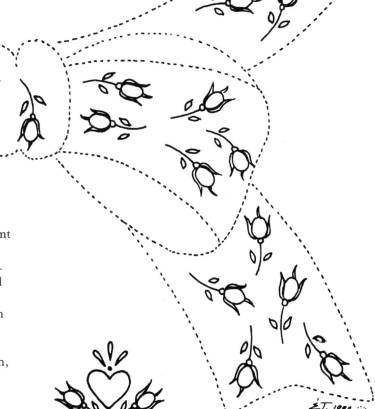

2. *Collar and pads:* Paint cream with #4 brush; also paint around eyes. Use two coats.
3. *Rosebuds:* Double load pale pink and cream, paint with #1 brush.
4. *Hearts:* Paint straight pink colour with #1 brush.
5. *Leaves:* Paint leaves with #00 brush, double load pale green and cream.
6. *Eyes:* Paint first dark brown with #2 brush, then paint centre of eyes black; when dry highlight with white.
7. *Nose:* Paint nose solid dark brown with #2 brush, highlight with white.
8. *Eyebrows and mouth:* With #00 brush paint fine dark brown lines. (Note: on some terracotta bears eyes and noses are already painted.)

Terracotta Pots

(illustrated inside back cover)

Materials

2 small, 1 medium and 1 large terracotta pots with saucers.

Paints: Waterbased acrylics
Brushes: #4, #2, #1, #00 round brushes
½'' and 1'' flat brushes
Tracing paper, transfer paper
Varnish: Polyurethane gloss finish
Pencils: 2B and 5H
Sandpaper: Wet-and-dry #400 or #600

Palette

Base coat: antique blue
Leaves: Dark green + white
Strawberries: Dark red + light red + yellow + white
Strawberry seeds: Yellow + white + black
Strawberry flowers: Light green + dark green + white
Curlicues: Rich gold
Duck: Grey + white
Bow and beak: Red + rich gold
Cheek: Red + white
Eye: Black + white, dots around eye black
Dot flowers: White

Preparation

Refer to page 3.

Painting guide
STRAWBERRIES

Painting guide is the same for all pots, except that #2 and #00 brushes are required for small pots.

1. *Leaves:* Paint all leaves with #4 or #2 brush, double loaded with dark green and white.
2. *Strawberries:* Paint strawberries first in dark red, let dry. Double load brush with dark red and light red, adding a touch of white—paint outer sides of strawberries. Next stroke, double load dark red and light red, add a touch of yellow and paint inner part of strawberry; fill in rest with red only.
3. *Strawberry seeds:* Paint teardrop strokes with #00 brush double loaded with yellow and white; add fine brown lines on one side of teardrops for shade.
4. *Strawberry flowers:* Paint flowers light green first, using #1 or #00 brush, then go over petals with white, using dry brush effect. Let dry.
   Paint all flower centres dark green, dots in yellow with #00 brush.
5. *Curlicues:* Paint all curlicues in rich gold with #00 brush.

Painting guide
DUCK

1. *Duck:* Paint duck with grey first with #4 brush; let dry.
2. *Paint over duck* with white only, using #4 brush; load brush well with white so each stroke shows movement to indicate feathers.
3. *Bow and cheek:* Paint with #2 brush, double load dark red with rich gold.
4. *Cheek:* Paint tiny dots in red with #00 brush, highlight with white.
5. *Eye:* Black, paint with #00 brush, also fine dots around eye.
6. *Dot flowers:* Paint white, use #00 brush.

Finish

Apply 1 coat of gloss finish polyurethane varnish with 1'' flat brush. Let dry, preferably overnight. Apply second coat of varnish.

Note

It is best not to plant direct into painted terracotta pots, as with frequent watering terracotta absorbs moisture which can result in your design peeling off the outside. To stop this I usually varnish my pots inside or seal them inside with all-purpose sealer (2 coats), or I place the plants into the pots in their original plastic containers. Once varnished pots will stand up well to heat or rain.

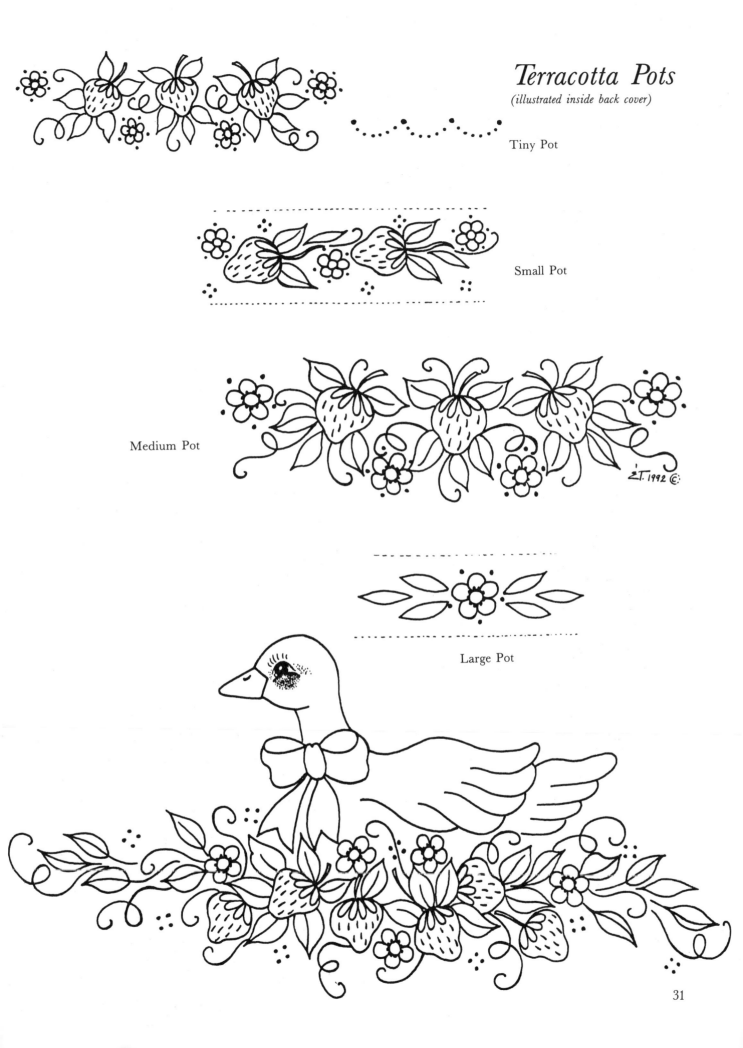

Terracotta Pots

(illustrated inside back cover)

Tiny Pot

Small Pot

Medium Pot

Large Pot

31

Small Gifts

(illustrated on front cover)

Materials

Terracotta basket, soap dish, potpourri dish, picture and picture frame.

Brushes: #4, #2, #1, #00 round brushes
Other materials same as for terracotta pots on page 30.

Palette

For all four articles.
Base coat: Pale lilac blue
Leaves: Dark green + light green + white
Violet: Mauve + lilac + Diox purple
Violet centre: White + orange
Curlicues: Dark green + rich gold

Painting guide

1. *Leaves:* Paint leaves dark green and light green with #4 brush. Add a touch of white to highlight.
2. *Violet:* Paint with #2 brush, mauve first, then add lilac and purple. Highlight with white.
3. *Violet centres:* Use #00 brush, paint white and orange.
4. *Curlicues:* Paint dark green, highlight with gold.
5. *Commas, lines:* Rich gold, use #00 brush.
6. *Basket:* Paint dark yellow first; use #2 brush, add light brown and dark brown next, highlight with white.
7. *Bow:* Purple and rich gold—double load #00 brush. Highlight basket with a touch of rich gold.

Finish

Apply 2 coats of satin finish polyurethane. Varnish with 1'' flat brush. Let dry between coats.